From Morn to Midnight

For B.

The compiler, illustrator and publishers would like to thank the following for permission to reproduce the poems in this book: Mr Richard Lester for 'A Cello'; Mrs Rosemary Pepler for lines from 'Concerning Dragons' by Hilary Pepler; Oxford University Press for eight lines from 'The Clifftop' from *The Poetical Works of Robert Bridges*; Oxford University Press for 'The night will never stay' and 'Nine o'clock bell' by Eleanor Farjeon. 'The Rivals' ('I heard a bird at dawn') is reprinted from *Collected Poems* by James Stephens, by permission of Mrs Iris Wise, Macmillan London and Basingstoke, and The Macmillan Company of Canada Limited. 'I am the sister of him' is reprinted by permission of G P Putnam's Sons from *Everything and Anything* by Dorothy Aldis. Copyright 1925, 1926, 1927 by Dorothy Aldis; renewed.

Library of Congress Cataloging in Publication Data

Main entry under title: From morn to midnight.

SUMMARY: Poems that are traditional or by famous authors explore the everyday world of children.
1. Children's poetry, English. [1. English poetry— Collections] I. Ichikawa, Satomi. II. Moss, Elaine.
PZ8.3.F927 821'.008 77-2548
ISBN 0-690-01393-0 ISBN 0-690-01394-9 (lib. bdg.)

From Morn to Midnight

SATOMI ICHIKAWA

Children's verses chosen by Elaine Moss

Thomas Y. Crowell Company
New York

The night will never stay,
The night will still go by,
Though with a million stars
You pin it to the sky;
Though you bind it with the blowing wind
And buckle it with the moon,
The night will slip away
Like sorrow or a tune.

ELEANOR FARJEON

The year's at the spring,
And day's at the morn;
Morning's at seven;
The hillside's dew-pearled;
The lark's on the wing;
The snail's on the thorn;
God's in his heaven—
All's right with the world!

ROBERT BROWNING

I heard a bird at dawn
Singing sweetly on a tree,
That the dew was on the lawn,
And the wind was on the lea;
But I didn't listen to him,
For he didn't sing to me!

I didn't listen to him,
For he didn't sing to me
That the dew was on the lawn,
And the wind was on the lea!
I was singing at the time
Just as prettily as he!

I was singing all the time,
Just as prettily as he,
About the dew upon the lawn,
And the wind upon the lea!
So I didn't listen to him,
As he sang upon a tree!

JAMES STEPHENS

My
cello big and fat
makes
the sound
of a screeching
rat. It plays F
double sharp
when I want
it to play
B flat. It
sounds like
a bad com-
position when
I play in the 4th
position. If I try
to play vibrato my
bow goes all
s-t-a-c-c-
ato
!

RICHARD
LESTER

I am the sister of him
And he is my brother,
But he is too little for us to
Talk to each other;
So every morning I show him
My doll and my book,
But every morning he still is
Too little to look.

DOROTHY ALDIS

Nine-o'Clock Bell!
Nine-o'Clock Bell!
All the small children and big ones as well,
Pulling their stockings up, snatching their hats,
Cheeking and grumbling and giving back-chats,
Laughing and quarrelling, dropping their things,
These at a snail's pace and those upon wings,
Lagging behind a bit, running ahead,
Waiting at corners for lights to turn red,
Some of them scurrying,
Others not worrying,
Carelessly trudging or anxiously hurrying,
All through the streets they are coming pell-mell
　　At the Nine-o'Clock
　　　　Nine-o'Clock
　　　　Nine-o'Clock
　　　　　　Bell!

ELEANOR
FARJEON

Bring the comb and play upon it!
  Marching, here we come!
Willie cocks his highland bonnet,
  Johnnie beats the drum.

Mary Jane commands the party,
  Peter leads the rear;
Feet in time, alert and hearty,
  Each a Grenadier!

All in the most martial manner
  Marching double-quick;
While the napkin like a banner
  Waves upon the stick!

Here's enough of fame and pillage,
  Great commander Jane!
Now that we've been round the village,
  Let's go home again.

ROBERT LOUIS STEVENSON

Where the pools are bright and deep,
Where the grey trout lies asleep,
Up the river and over the lea,
That's the way for Billy and me.

Where the blackbird sings the latest,
Where the hawthorn blooms the sweetest,
Where the nestlings chirp and flee,
That's the way for Billy and me.

Where the mowers mow the cleanest,
Where the hay lies thick and greenest,
There to track the homeward bee,
That's the way for Billy and me.

Where the hazel bank is steepest,
Where the shadow falls the deepest,
Where the clustering nuts fall free,
That's the way for Billy and me.

Why the boys should drive away
Little sweet maidens from their play,
Or love to banter and fight so well,
That's a thing I never could tell.

But this I know, I love to play
Through the meadow, among the hay;
Up the water and over the lea,
That's the way for Billy and me.

JAMES HOGG

Found in the garden—dead in his beauty.
  Ah, that a linnet should die in the spring!
Bury him, comrades, in pitiful duty,
  Muffle the dinner bell, solemnly ring.

Bury him kindly—up in the corner;
  Bird, beast, and goldfish are sepulchred there.
Bid the black kitten march as chief mourner,
  Waving her tail like a plume in the air.

Bury him nobly—next to the donkey;
  Fetch the old banner, and wave it about.
Bury him deeply—think of the monkey,
  Shallow his grave, and the dogs got him out.

Bury him softly—white wool around him,
  Kiss his poor feathers—the first kiss and last;
Tell his poor widow kind friends have found him:
  Plant his poor grave with whatever grows fast.

Farewell, sweet singer! dead in thy beauty,
  Silent through summer, though other birds sing.
Bury him, comrades, in pitiful duty,
  Muffle the dinner bell, mournfully ring.

                    JULIANA HORATIA EWING

Every child who has gardening tools,
Should learn by heart these gardening rules:

He who owns a gardening spade,
Should be able to dig the depth of its blade.

He who owns a gardening rake,
Should know what to leave and what to take.

He who owns a gardening hoe,
Must be sure how he means his strokes to go.

But he who owns a gardening fork,
May make it do all the other tools' work.

Though to shift or to pot or annex what you can,
A trowel's the tool for child, woman, or man.

'Twas the bird that sits in the medlar-tree,
Who sang these gardening saws to me.

JULIANA HORATIA EWING

How do you like to go up in a swing,
Up in the air so blue?
Oh, I do think it the pleasantest thing
Ever a child can do!

Up in the air and over the wall,
Till I can see so wide,
Rivers and trees and cattle and all
Over the countryside—

Till I look down on the garden green,
Down on the roof so brown—
Up in the air I go flying again,
Up in the air and down!

ROBERT LOUIS STEVENSON

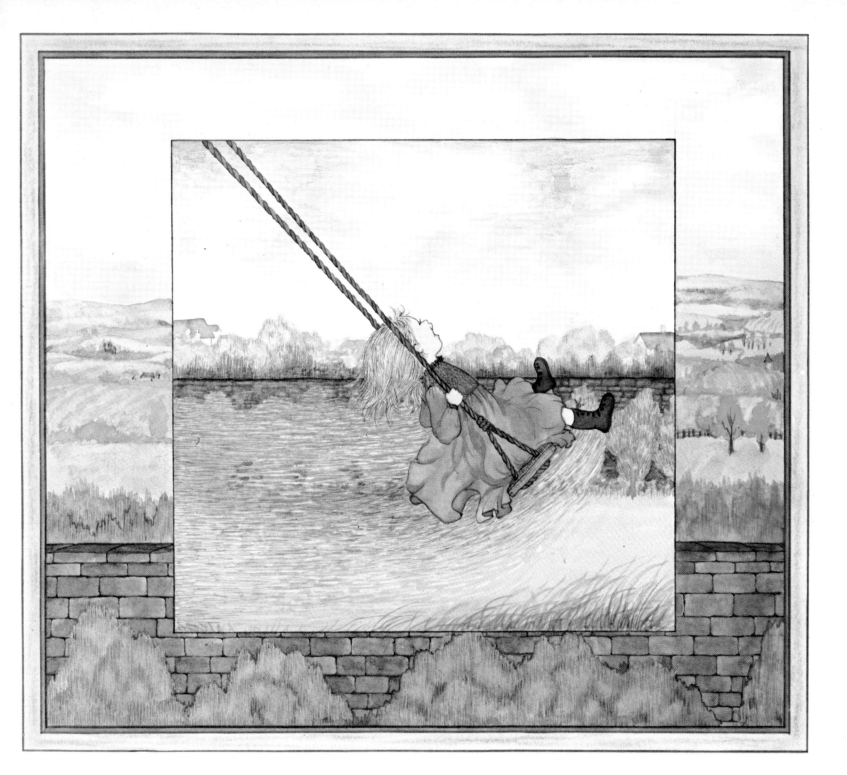

The cliff-top has a carpet
  Of lilac, gold and green:
The blue sky bounds the ocean
  The white clouds scud between.

A flock of gulls are wheeling
  And wailing round my seat;
Above my head the heaven,
  The sea beneath my feet.

ROBERT BRIDGES

Little Johnny fished all day,
Fishes would not come his way.
"Had enough of this," said he,
"I'll be going home to tea!"

When the fishes saw him go,
Up they came all in a row;
Jumped about and laughed with glee,
Shouting "Johnny's gone to tea!"

TRADITIONAL

Little children skip,
The rope so gaily gripping,
Tom and Harry,
Jane and Mary,
Kate, Diana,
Susan, Anna,
All are fond of skipping!

The grasshoppers all skip,
The early dewdrop sipping,
Under, over
Bent and clover,
Daisy, sorrel,
Without quarrel,
All are fond of skipping!

The little boats they skip,
Beside the heavy shipping,
And while the squalling
Winds are calling,
Falling, rising,
Rising, falling,
All are fond of skipping!

The autumn leaves they skip,
When blasts the trees are stripping:
Bounding, whirling,
Sweeping, twirling
And in wanton mazes curling,
All are fond of skipping!

THOMAS HOOD

When the voices of children are heard on the green
And laughing is heard on the hill,
My heart is at rest within my breast
And everything else is still.

"Then come home, my children, the sun is gone down,
And the dews of night arise;
Come, come, leave off play, and let us away
Till the morning appears in the skies."

"No, no, let us play, for it is yet day
And we cannot go to sleep;
Besides, in the sky the little birds fly,
And the hills are all covered with sheep."

"Well, well, go and play till the light fades away,
And then go home to bed."
The little ones leaped and shouted and laughed
And all the hills echoèd.

WILLIAM BLAKE

In jumping and tumbling
We spend the whole day,
Till night by arriving
Has finished our play.

What then? One and all,
There's no more to be said,
As we tumbled all day,
So we tumble to bed.

TRADITIONAL

When my brother Tommy
Sleeps in bed with me
He doubles up
And makes
himself
exactly
like
a
V

And 'cause the bed is not so wide
A part of him is on my side.

ABRAM BUNN ROSS

The sun descending in the west,
The evening star does shine;
The birds are silent in their nest,
And I must seek for mine.
The moon, like a flower,
In heaven's high bower,
With silent delight
Sits and smiles on the night.

WILLIAM BLAKE

Said the Wind to the Moon,
"I will blow you out;
   You stare
   In the air
   Like a ghost in a chair
Always looking what I am about.
I hate to be watched—I'll blow you out."

GEORGE MACDONALD

Are all the dragons dead
And all the witches fled?
Am I quite safe in bed?

HILARY PEPLER